Patrick's Wish

Written by Karen Mitchell with Rebecca Upjohn
Photographs provided by Patrick4Life

Second Story Press

My big brother Patrick had a wish. For a long time he kept it secret, so I didn't know. I just knew he loved to play, and he would play with me.

"Come on Lyanne, let's go!" And we'd be out the door in a flash. Some brothers don't want their little sisters tagging along, but not Patrick. "I have tons of friends. You're one too."

That made me happy.

This is Patrick.

And this is me, Lyanne,
when I was just a kid.

Sometimes before we went out, Patrick had to have a needle. He was born with a bleeding disorder called hemophilia. It meant if he got a cut or bruise he would bleed for a long time because his blood couldn't clot. Some bleeding happened inside his body. To help the bleeding stop, he needed other people's blood. He got that blood into his body through a needle in the vein of his hand.

But that was just the way it was with Patrick. I didn't think about it much.

You can see that when Patrick was very young, he would bruise easily.

In winter if we weren't skating or cross-country skiing, we'd race on the toboggan hill.

"How do we go faster?" I loved the feeling of the wind in my face as we swooped down the slope.

Patrick would show me even though he might get bruises or bleeding in his joints that hurt so much. Nothing stopped him from doing what he wanted or trying something new, so nothing stopped me either.

I had to try really hard to keep up with him. He was good at *everything*.

Our mom is a piano teacher so there was a lot of music in our house.

"Hey Lyanne, come help me with this."

I'd scoot onto the piano bench beside Patrick.

"You do this part." He'd show me some chords to play over and over. "And I'll do this." He'd play with me but using different notes so we were in harmony.

Together we sounded just right.

"What's it called?" Mom asked once.

Patrick gave his big soft smile. "Patrick and Lyanne's masterpiece."

"That's a silly title," I said.

"What would you call it?" asked Patrick.

"Lyanne and Patrick's masterpiece, of course."

Patrick laughed pretty hard and then gave me a hug. I don't know why. He just did things like that.

And then one day everything changed. It was the day I found out about Patrick's wish. Mom and Dad said I was old enough to know. We all sat at the table: Mom, Dad, Patrick, my other brother Richard, and me.

Patrick sat next to me. His smile was gone. "Lyanne, I have a secret that I've been keeping for a while."

Everyone looked so serious. I didn't like it. What secret?

Mom told me that because Patrick needed so much blood for his hemophilia, it had to come from many people. But some of the blood he had used carried a virus in it called HIV. Mom said it like the letters "H-I-V". Then she said that Patrick had the virus now too. It was in his blood.

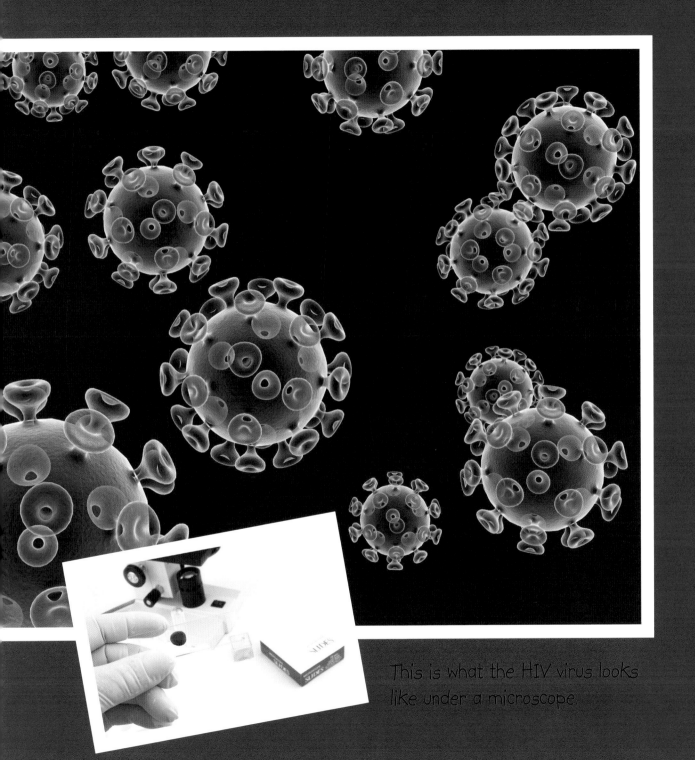

This is what the HIV virus looks like under a microscope.

I didn't understand right away. I knew a virus made you sick, like the flu or a cold. But then it went away and you got better. But Mom and Dad told me that HIV was serious and that it doesn't go away. It makes it hard for your body to fight infection. And one day HIV develops into AIDS. For now, Patrick would be fine, but when his HIV turned to AIDS, his body wouldn't be able to get well again. There isn't any cure.

I felt tears falling and I couldn't stop them. The blood was supposed to help him! How could it take away his life instead? I didn't want to know his secret. All I could do was cry and feel afraid. And then Patrick was there. He just held me until I had no more tears. I felt his arms around me. He smelled the same and felt the same, and he looked like Patrick. He was still my same big brother.

For a long time, you couldn't even tell that anything was wrong with Patrick.

He said that now I was his secret-keeper along with Mom, Dad, and Richard.

Then he told me about his wish. "I wish for a cure for AIDS," he said. "Lyanne, I'm not the only one with HIV. Will you wish with me?"

So every month on the full moon we made that wish together. We wished that before the next full moon, a cure for AIDS would be found.

Besides making a wish every month, Patrick and I would participate in AIDS awareness walks because we wanted to help find a cure for AIDS.

Patrick went away sometimes. Mom said he had to have regular check-ups with the doctors in the city. Patrick told me he didn't mind. "They are really friendly in the hospital, Lyanne." He wanted to be an emergency doctor some day.

Sometimes he did things alone with Dad or with Richard. They played golf and tennis and went snowmobiling. Sometimes we all went on family trips like to the Baseball Hall of Fame or Disneyland. We often went to the cottage where we would swim and play cards or draw. And sometimes he did things with just me.

Patrick took Pico, our Dalmatian, with him everywhere he could. "She's special, Lyanne. I can tell her anything, no matter how I feel."

Patrick kept on doing what he always did. He never let his secret stop him. So I didn't either. He made me laugh. He laughed with lots of people. That was Patrick.

This is Patrick with Pico

and at Disneyland!

One day he said he wanted to share his secret with the whole world. He said people were afraid of HIV and AIDS. He wanted them to hear the truth. First, he told our grandparents and the rest of the family. Then he told his friends. Then he told his school. He told them all about his secret, and he told them his wish.

Most people listened. Some people cried. Some people wanted to help. And some people were afraid. One of my friends wasn't allowed to come to my house and play anymore. Her family was afraid that she would catch HIV. Mom explained that it wasn't easy to become infected. You can't get it from playing together. But her family was too scared to listen and she stopped being my friend. It made me sad. And it made me mad. People who are sick need more help from their friends not less.

One after another, Patrick told friends and family about his secret.

But Patrick didn't let what people said or thought stop him. His wish grew and grew because more people shared it now. He talked to many students about the virus and how they could protect themselves from it.

When Patrick got too sick to walk far on his own, I pushed his wheelchair. We still went out together. At the lake, we watched the waves spray into the air. It smelled fresh. If I closed my eyes, it felt like the wind whooshing in our faces on the toboggan hill.

Even in the wheelchair, Patrick liked to go places!

"You know it's too late now for my wish to come true for me, don't you, Lyanne?" Patrick said one day.

"It will!" I said. I didn't want to hear. I didn't want to think about my big brother not being with me. But it was Patrick, who always told the truth, so I listened.

"Will you keep making my wish, Lyanne? I hope someday there will be a cure for AIDS, but for now people have to learn the truth about it so they can stop being afraid. Then they can protect themselves. When I'm not here anymore, will you tell my story so that one day no more brothers or sisters or mothers or fathers or friends will get sick from this terrible disease? I wish for no more AIDS!"

I promised my big brother that I would.

And now Patrick's wish is mine to share with you.

Some Things Patrick Would Want You To Know About HIV and AIDS:

1. HIV means Human Immunodeficiency Virus.
It is a germ that affects people by attacking the cells in their body that fight infection.

AIDS means Acquired Immunodeficiency Syndrome.
It is a group of illnesses that people can get when the fighter cells in their body are worn down and they can no longer fight infection.

2. It is very hard for children to get HIV/AIDS.
You cannot get it from going to school with someone who has it.
You cannot get HIV/AIDS from playing, living, or working with someone who has it.
You cannot get it from a sneeze, a cough, or sharing dishes or snacks.
You cannot get it from a toilet seat, a doorknob, a swimming pool, a bug bite, or a pet.
You cannot catch it from napping with someone who has it or from a hug, a kiss, or from their clothes.

3. HIV/AIDS is carried in the blood. The virus cannot live outside the human body for long.

4. You can't tell if people have HIV just by looking at them.

5. You can't get HIV from giving blood or from getting needles at the doctor's office.

6. In North America and many countries today, it is nearly impossible to become infected with HIV from donated blood. These days, before it is given to anyone, donated blood is tested to make sure it doesn't carry HIV. Sadly, Patrick was getting his blood donations before there was a test for HIV and some people at that time were infected like Patrick.

7. People with HIV and AIDS are like you and me. When they get sick they need care and help from family and friends the way the rest of us do. You cannot become infected with HIV/AIDS from caring for someone who has it.

8. In the last few years, researchers have discovered drugs that have stopped HIV from becoming AIDS in some people. Medical scientists are still working hard to find a cure.

9. At the moment, there is no vaccine. There is still no cure. But you can prevent it from happening to you. Learn how to protect yourself.

And most of all, Patrick would want you to remember his wish:

No more HIV/AIDS.